Christmas

Lori Dittmer

seedlings

CREATIVE EDUCATION • CREATIVE PAPERBACKS

Published by Creative Education and Creative Paperbacks
P.O. Box 227, Mankato, Minnesota 56002
Creative Education and Creative Paperbacks
are imprints of The Creative Company
www.thecreativecompany.us

Design by Ellen Huber; production by Colin O'Dea
Art direction by Rita Marshall
Printed in China

Photographs by Getty Images (Per Breiehagen/The Image Bank, daitoZen/Moment, Vstock LLC/Vstock), iStockphoto (~UserGI15633745, cclickclick, eli_asenova, evgenyatamanenko, gleitfrosch, imtmphoto, inhauscreative, jakkapan21, jgroup, knape, loops7, Magone, Pink_frog, ryasick, SolStock, David Tran, Vitalina, ZoneCreative), Shutterstock (gkrphoto)

Library of Congress Cataloging-in-Publication Data
Names: Dittmer, Lori, author.
Title: Christmas / Lori Dittmer.
Series: Seedlings.
Includes index.
Summary: A kindergarten-level introduction to Christmas, covering the holiday's history, popular traditions, and such defining symbols as evergreen trees and gifts.
Identifiers: LCCN 2019053281 / ISBN 978-1-64026-325-3 (hardcover) / ISBN 978-1-62832-857-8 (pbk) / ISBN 978-1-64000-455-9 (eBook)
Subjects: LCSH: Christmas—Juvenile literature.
Classification: LCC GT4985.5.D57 2020 / DDC 394.261—dc23

CCSS: RI.K.1, 2, 3, 4, 5, 6, 7;
RI.1.1, 2, 3, 4, 5, 6, 7; RF.K.1, 3; RF.1.1

First Edition HC 9 8 7 6 5 4 3 2 1
First Edition PBK 9 8 7 6 5 4 3 2 1

TABLE OF CONTENTS

Hello, Christmas!

Christmas is a time of joy. It marks the birth of Jesus Christ.

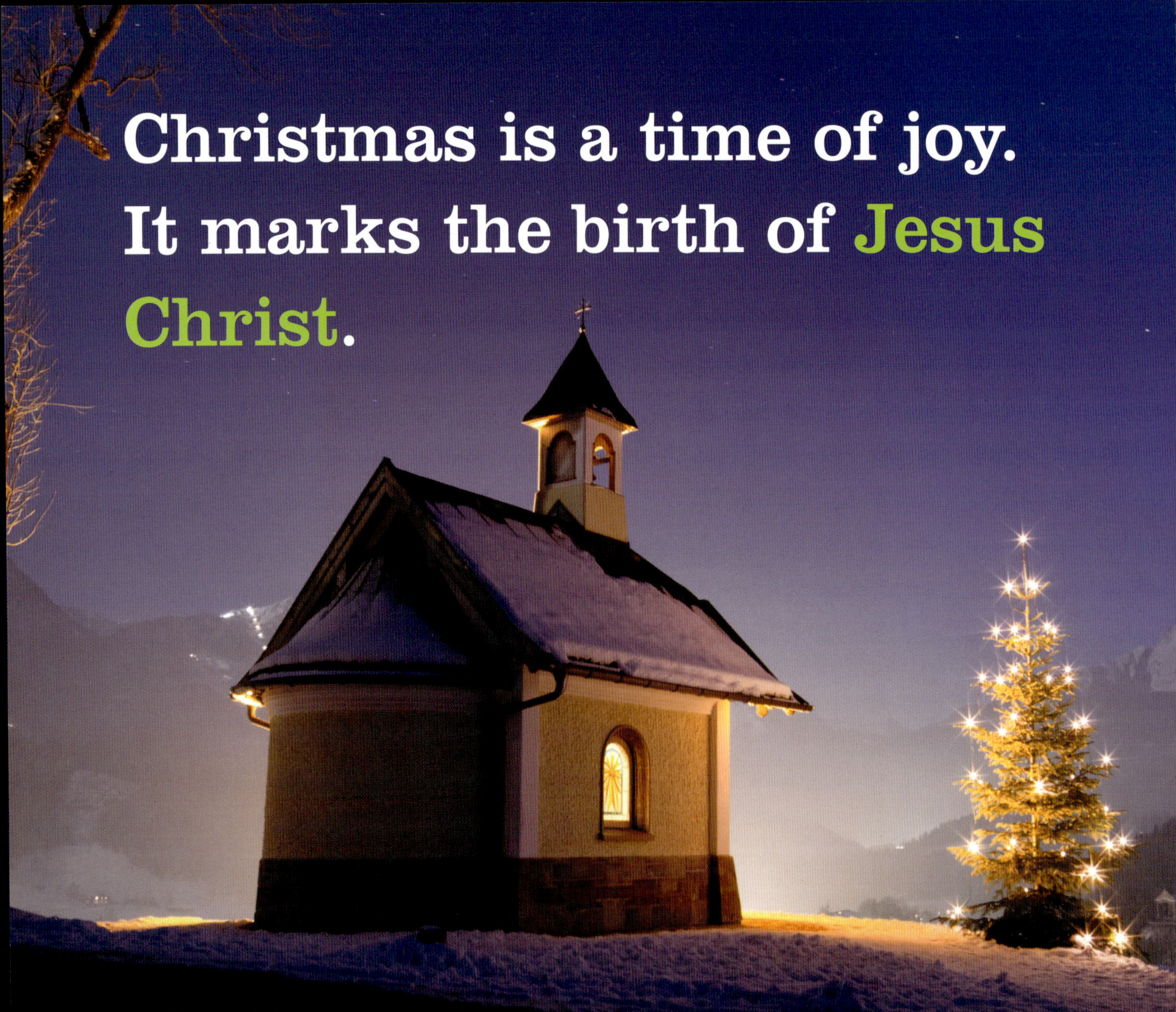

People around the world celebrate on December 25.

Many people put up an **evergreen** tree.

They string lights on it.

People who studied the stars brought gifts to baby Jesus.

This is one reason Christmas is a time for gifts.

Stories of a man who brought gifts to people were told in many places.

He was called St. Nicholas, Father Christmas, or Santa Claus.

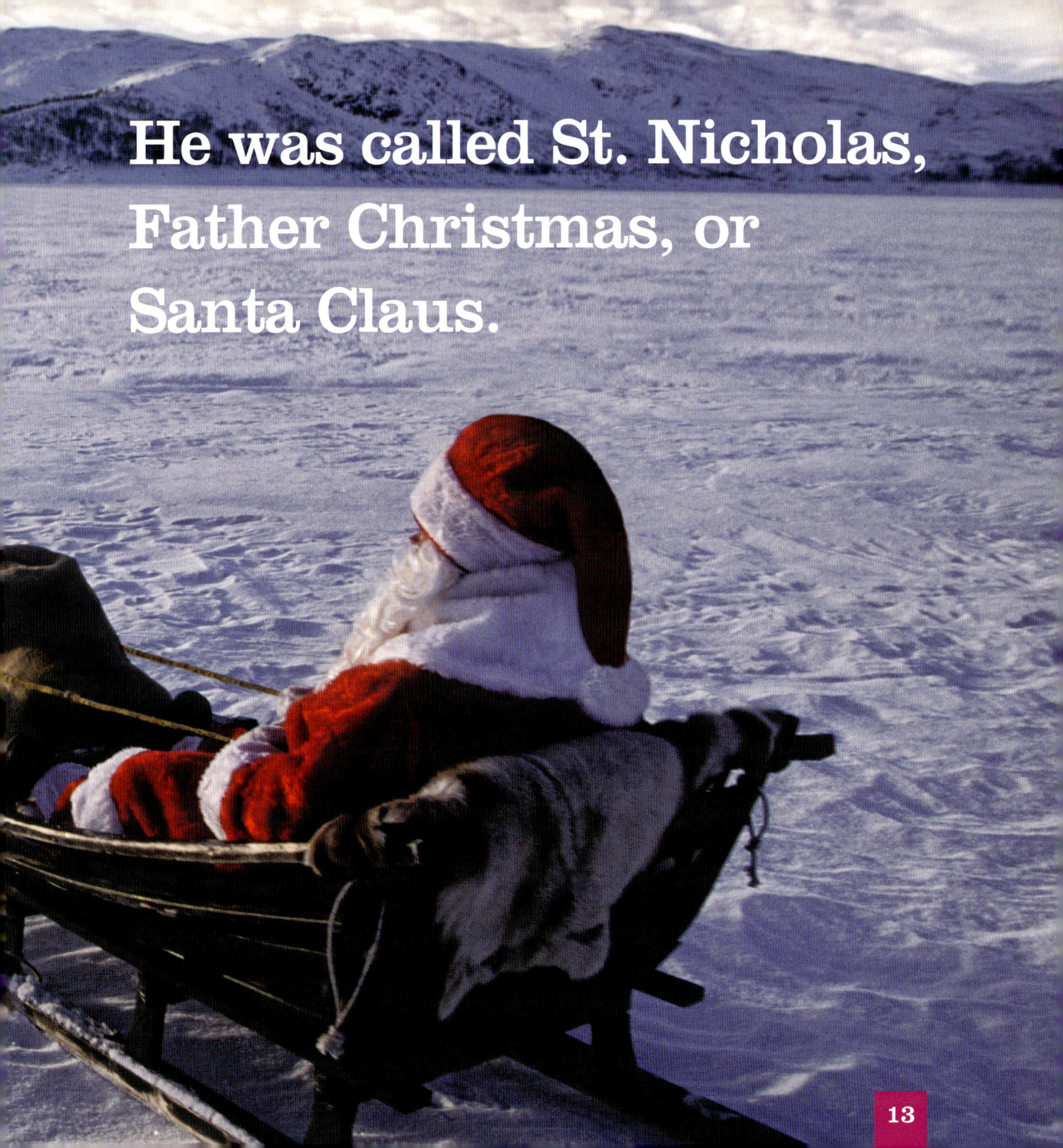

Special Christmas foods might include fruitcake or mince pie.

Some people bake cookies. They eat them with friends.

People give gifts.
They sing carols.

They eat big meals together.

Goodbye, Christmas!

Picture Christmas

nativity

lights

Santa Claus

Christmas tree

Words to Know

carols: songs of praise or joy, usually sung at Christmas

evergreen: a tree or plant that stays green all year

Jesus Christ: the man whom Christians believe was the son of God

mince: a finely chopped mixture used as pie filling

Read More

Grack, Rachel. *Christmas.*
Minneapolis: Bellwether Media, 2017.

Rustad, Martha E. H. *All About Christmas.*
North Mankato, Minn.: Capstone Press, 2016.

Websites

Ducksters Holidays – Christmas
https://www.ducksters.com/holidays/christmas.php
Find out some fun facts, and learn to say "Merry Christmas" in other languages.

Why Christmas: We Answer Your Christmas Questions!
https://www.whychristmas.com
Learn more about the Christmas story and how people around the world celebrate.

Index